"Wait for me," called Ray.
But the kids were way ahead.

It was like this every day.

Ray kept trying.

But he could not keep up.

Wait for Me

by Sidney Allen
illustrated by Diane Paterson

Core Decodable 81

McGraw Hill Education

Bothell, WA • Chicago, IL • Columbus, OH • New York, NY

MHEonline.com

McGraw-Hill Education

Send all inquiries to:
McGraw-Hill Education
8787 Orion Place
Columbus, OH 43240

ISBN: 978-0-02-143388-9
MHID: 0-02-143388-7

Printed in the United States of America.

7 8 9 LCR 25 24 23

This time, the kids stopped on the corner.
But they came right back.

The kids passed Ray.
Ray turned his bike.
"Wait for me," he called.

Why was Ray always far back?
His bike still had training wheels.

That night, Ray was sad.

"Why do you feel bad?" Dad asked.

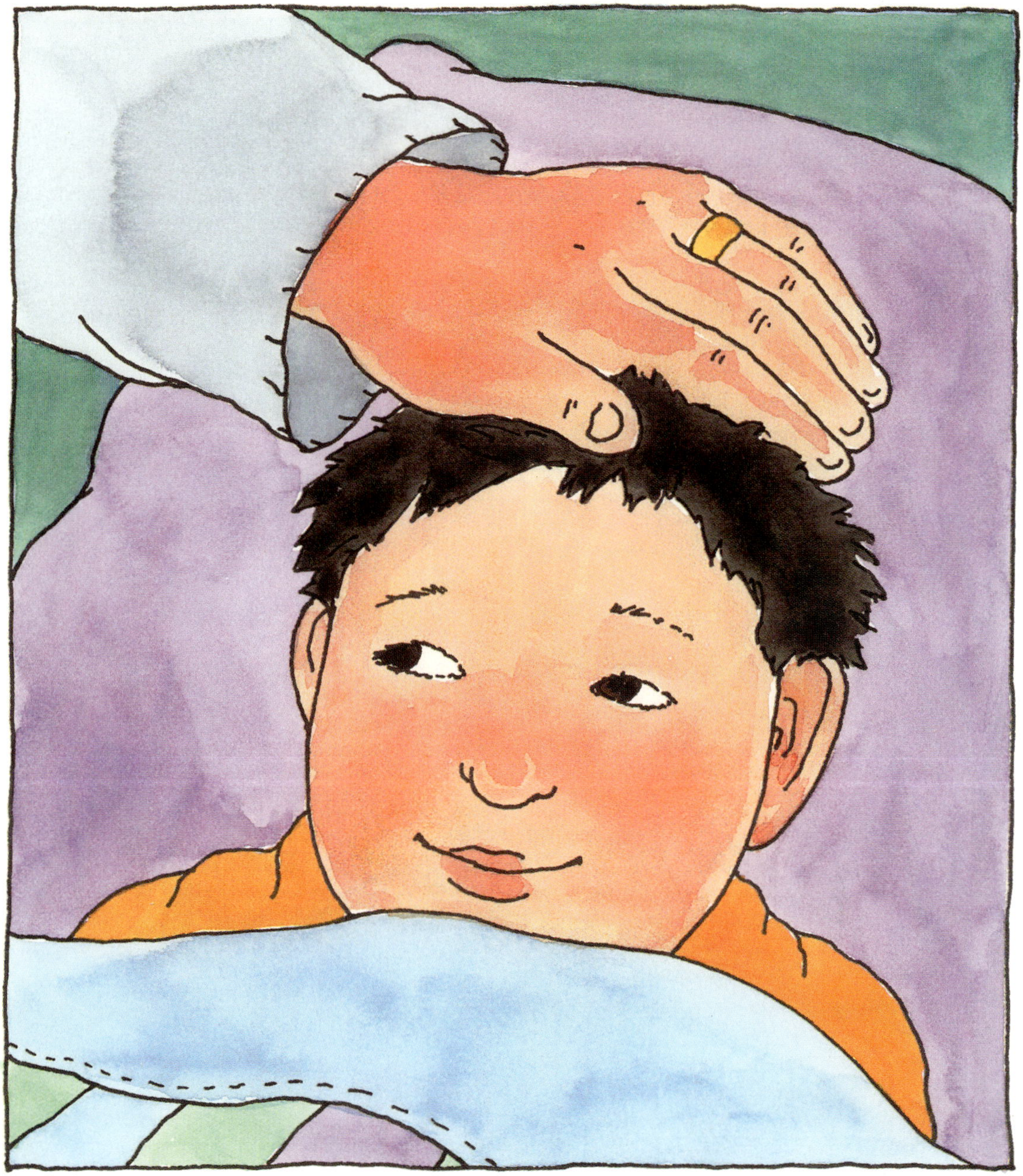

"I cannot ride fast," said Ray.
"My bike still has training wheels."
"We can fix that," said Dad.

The next day, Dad called Ray.
"Go to the driveway," said Dad.

Ray spotted his bike in the bright sun.
It did not have training wheels!

Ray was glad.
But he was a little afraid.
He might need training wheels.

"Try riding this way," said Dad.
Dad held the bike as Ray pedaled.
Dad ran next to him.

Ray pedaled fast.
Dad let the bike go.
Could Ray tell?

Ray was riding alone.
"I am flying, Dad!" he yelled.

That day, the kids raced.
Ray stayed with them.
It was a tie!